CAMINANTE

First Edition

ISBN 1-903110-12-2

Cover Design Owen Benwell

Published in 2003 by
Wrecking Ball Press
9 Westgate • North Cave • Brough • East Yorkshire • HU15 2NG

Milner Place

CAMINANTE

Acknowledgements

...are due to the editors of the following magazines:

Ambit, Brando's Hat, Draft2, Dream Catcher, London Magazine, Pennine Platform, Poetry Review, the rue bella, Sheffield Thursday, The Wide Skirt. some poems also appeared in the Confusion of Anglers and Where Smoke Is, from Wide Skirt Press. The poems Piltdown Man and Bat Woman were first published by SPOUT Publications.

Author's note

The reasons that I chose to use a Spanish word as the title for this selection were not only to recognize my debt to Hispanic culture and poets, especially Lorca, Neruda, Miguel Hernandez, but also for the significance to me of two lines from Antonio Machado that were also the inspiration for one of my early poems, The Navvy; *Caminante no hay camino / se hace camino al andar - Traveller there is no road / the road is made as you go.*

This seems not only a whole philosophy in two brief lines, but also exemplifies for me how poems arrive and the adventure they become.

For the rest I will just leave this:

> I am the echo
> of those books
> upon the wall.
> I am the offspring
> of the hands
> that laid these stones.
> This wind upon my cheek I know
> and the dead petal
> at its fall.

Contents

THE NAVVY

Caminante, no hay camino
se hace camino al andar...*
                    Antonio Machado

for the navigator
the pick
is familiar
as a violet in the gutter
sea opening
between mountains' thighs
hands calloused
                    by swing
of axe even
the softest footsteps
blister

bridges
along this highway
cross
the gathering of dew
and the road reaches
as far
as the eye
will
see

* Traveller, there is no road
  the road is made as you go...

THE MAN WHO HAD FORGOTTEN
THE NAMES OF TREES.

I am not ashamed of dying
nor of arguments with the sea's skin
that are quickly resolved, nor of ignorance
of the ancestry of unlikely fish, teeming
where the rocks wedge the cold currents,
stem their appointments with dissipation.

No I am not ashamed of dying.

A woman I met in a sad garden,
when the moon had three rings
and the wind smelled of great horses,
told me her secret name but left me
before I had learned its distant origins.

But bending over a fire, nourishing
flour with fierce hands, smuggling
her wisdom past the guards in sailor suits
and dog-collars, she inherits a world
of incense and the reek of cordite.

Whenever an anticyclone dawdles in January
and soil returns to rock, the morning
air to water, and I am not amused,
I look for her in the mist.

And there she is.

Sometimes only a shadow like a moth
or a postman,
sometimes a faraway song
that smells of rags
scrape of a worn shoe,
brush of a velvet cuff on my cheek.
Bracing myself as the earth rolls,

I lean against the north,
look into a sky gone blue
for the coming of wistful birds.

And there she is.

Her secret name is an hour-long kiss.

To return to where I wasn't,
I see a man with a gap-toothed rake
in the hayfield, numbed by the pain
of fragile monotony, glancing
from time to another time
up to the idle park and the great house
on the hill. The armourers
are wiping their hands on their aprons.
The banker is smiling. No

I'm not ashamed of dying.

IT'S TEN TO TEN IN THE GREY HORSE

and the majority are only drinking
out of habit. It's hardly
the high-spot for bacchanalians;
the barmaid's indifferent, beer
undistinguished and a thin man
in the corner is having a fit.

If it were a postcard or a particular
kind of painting, when the village clock
struck the appointed hour
the men would drag themselves
to their cottages to sleep
under the thatch where the women
dream of an ocean of hollyhocks.

But the man with fits
sleeps in a flat above a garage

14

and has no coins for the meter.
He is dying quicker than most
of asbestosis and his inheritance.
Come to think of it
he may be luckier than some.

When I am thrown out, I pause
by some graves and listen
for a warm sea and birds
that have no roost. The shore
swarms with white crabs that click
when they scavenge under constellations
that would have confused Babylonian astronomers.
They have to make a living too.

Tall skinny trees bend
to an incessant wind.
What's-his-name is nowhere to be seen.
His wife snores under a sapodilly, gorged
on its rough-skinned fruit.

Tonight I prefer mountains,
stumble ashore with a machete
to hack a path through the sea-grapes
and the poison-wood thickets
to the pampas. Having no fear
of gauchos, I rope a passing horse.

The horizon enlarges.
The agonies of a city
are by-passed and a breeze
that tumbles from the west dispels
the groans of childbirth and gamblers.
Some way ahead I can hear
a great silence and spur the horse
towards its springs.
I sleep in a pillaged tomb.
I 'VE CLEAN FORGOTTEN TO TELL YOU THAT

before I waded to the shore, before
we even smelled the land and watched
the changing of the birds,
we passed a rock shaped like a sunfish fin
but blacker than a raven's beak, and all
alone and weeping with the seas
that broke on it like a metronome.
You'd think they'd find a handier spot
to stick such a pestilential rock.

Just when you think the ocean's clear,
no land to give you sleepless nights,
some rage in the body of the earth
thrusts up a putrid boil like this
to break ships' ribs, asphyxiate all hands.

I knew a man in Southport just like that.

THE TREES MARCH DOWN THE MOUNTAINS

like a Tartar horde, spears waving,
a billion shining shields flickering
in the sun, criss-crossed by shrieking birds
and in among the horses' legs
run packs of rabid dogs.

Actually, it is quite quiet in the forest,
and cool, the air has the warm scent
of disintegration, sweetness
of decay and fungi. The streams
are wick with eyes and lined
with listening ferns. Some of the silence
has trickled down from the mountains
but there is a crackling of beetles
and, farther than nearer, derisory monkeys.

16

Alas how is't with you,
That you do bend your eye on vacancy
And with th 'incorporal air do hold discourse?

Too bloody true

I WONDER IF SHE WATCHES NOW

perhaps from the branches of that thing
that breaks the sky and shit-white
with the droppings of loose birds
that sing their angry songs and wing
off at the crack of frost.

Soft as their down, perhaps she's watching
those rocks or from the fog pinched
from a passing cloud or that puny stream
tinkling like reprocessed beer.

I should have drunk much less last night.

THOUGH I AM DEAFER THAN A POPE

I hear her singing in the reeds
and in the morning mist beside
another river and the parrots fly
gilded in borrowed light above
the aspirations of the trees.

I hear her busking in the cold
angles of the streets; singing
of superannuated leaves and why
she has a pact with death she dedicates
to all her children, all those
who walk in shadows, through the doors
of pain and penitence, and such like
ordinary things that string the harp,
make glass the necklaces of queens.

17

Arbuthnot Lovely loves to say,
when in another's cups, that dying
is an absolute way of drowning those
who live in yesterday.

She whispers something in his ear;
something too true to mention here.

The seas arrive on time, visit the creeks
like farmers on market day, the moon
as multi-national as jeans or beans,
as constant as the chant of guns.

Skirts rustling through ripened wheat
she walks towards her waiting car.
A wind moans through a scrawny bush,
carrying her scent and a plover's cry,
gathering ash from a tinker's fire.

ONCE IN THE EMBERS OF A TIRESOME DAY

when starlings gathered for their autumn flight,
she came, and told me how the smoke of time curled round
the seven hills and how the ferryman stood patiently
beside his boat, whistling out of tune, and, smiling
like a drunken clown, asked if she'd pay by credit card.

She has a might of tales like that.

She tells of burning in the fire,
at stakes, on funeral pyres, in ovens
not designed for bread, of all the silences
condoned by holy men, and latticed
windows of hareems. Her silver laugh
shines like a nacre shell.

Once on a hill above a field of rape
as yellow as a lollipop, she sang

18

a bitter song of wounded knees
and calloused hands and how
a patriarchal god just condescends.
But then she smiled, patted my arm,
offered me her sea-blue eyes.

She has the power of water,
strength of sky.

LAST NIGHT WHEN ALL THE GOWNS

lay in their piles, the night air dripped
its dew and rats played their accustomed roles,
she rustled through the pale-faced streets,
danced round me as I wove to home.

She knows my desperation's in the blood,
my heart a weak-springed clock, my feet
drag down the road but I still grin
at my shadow and three-headed dogs.

The sun rode up, the streets began
to patter, vans arrived to empty, fill,
and newspapers came out, and she
went picking in the opening shops,

for fruit and flour, sugar and bras,
pigs' knuckles and perfumes.
She shimmered through a rising tide
of those who passed with vacant eyes.

JUNK MAIL, JUNK FOOD, I'LL BOARD A JUNK

to sail on a junket round the world, calling on
shores where hoopoes dance, flashing their combs,
and others where the elephant seals are copulating
and their roars are mocked by arctic terns.

19

My ship will visit Malabar, not Timbuctoo, it's not
a bloody camel. You can come along but only if
you promise not to screw my crew, or wear petunias
in your hair, sleep on watch, snort coke, sniff glue.

No need of that aboard my ship. The winds I ride
will send you higher than a sky-sail yard, the waters
from the wells of islands that I know, will drink you
drunker than a football crowd, blow up your mind

and from sunsets and variegated dawns you'll steal
the colours that a fire-crest wears to stimulate his mate,
and from the squawks of gulls and goony birds I'll score
you a symphony diviner than Mozart or Bach, or Brahms.

I know of ports so secret that their names are only
printed on the charts drawn by hydrographers disciplined
in necromancy and associated arts and kept in brassbound
chests secured by knots even Excalibur couldn't undo.

My compass has no card, we sail by stars and navigate
by day by following such birds we light on, and by night,
when clouds roll out a carpet, by the stench of land
lying beyond the horizon, or by the wake of whales.

This is the circumnavigation of a life, great circle
course over the swish-swash ocean of one time.

BUT THE BEER IN THE POTTER'S ARMS IS CLEAR

and cool. Swallows arrive to knife the air, the bees
to buzz and in the park the sleepers on the benches wake
each day a trifle earlier. Buses sail past the windows,
hearses sweep by and students rock to earphones. Gulls
scrap on refuse heaps like bishops, car horns make war
and gentles turn to bluebottles before your very eyes.
Pond-skaters scatter on the pond, kingfishers fish. Sunlight
lights on a satellite dish. I peer through an empty glass,
boot up the machine, tap in some sentences of my obituary.

She stands behind me, licks my ear

I KNOW SHE IS WATCHING

as I walk over the stubble
in the late sunlight.
She is aware
of the holes in my shoes.
I am not alone as I go towards the trees

She will be there
when the wind seizes my smoke.
She will carry my ash
to the mountains
for the rain to wash
to the sea.

ICE FLOW

for Alan Pascoc

*In 1845, Sir John Frank in and 128 men in the Terror and Erebus
sailed for the Arctic to search for the North West Passage. Over the
next three years every member of the expedition perished, leaving
their skeletons and pitiful artefacts scattered among the bleak
islands West of Baffin Bay. Most left their bones on a dreadful line of
march southwards, after the ships had been broken by the ice. But
the first three to die, William Braine, John Hartnell and John
Torrington, were buried on Beechey Island before the main disaster
struck.*

*Recently, these graves were opened and the bodies found to be almost
perfectly preserved in the permafrost. After being carefully examined
by doctors and scientists, the corpses were reinterred in their original
condition.*

I'll say this for them, they did
their very best. The coffin of mahogany,
wrapped in navy blue. I heard
their shuffling feet along the ice,

their heavy breathing, almost saw
their hard-fought dignity. I heard
the ringing picks that dug my pit,
screech of shovels on the snow,

the pious words that were for them
their epitaph among the floes and bergs.

*Do you talk riddles shit do you talk
riddles in this pit of piss ice
do you talk*

Some other day or year I woke,
if you can call it that, from a dreaming
of a bear. I swear I heard it scuffling

and snorting up topsides, clawing
and scraping at the snow and ice
that's all the seasons that we know,
that and the geese - they mind me
of that island in Baffin Bay, its ponds

harassed by Greylags, Barnacles and Brent,
a Saturday night of shiftless birds. Minds me
of Portsmouth in June, the Fleet in, and all
the girls in bloom, freckles and fancies.

John Benbow, that was his name, the lad
with buckled teeth, that played the flute,
with just one eye, and cried, and died
in Port o' Spain. His sister had a mole

just under the left ear and brittle hair.
Odd that the geese call reaches here.

Time was time has this ticking when
the colours gone gone along black
has a certain sparkling don't you think

Know what I think about a lot?
Sand in my shoes and its warm
irritation, like tea and currant

buns - it's more than that, it clings
to mortality, holds in its grains
the sun, the light that cozens

out the flowers: and with the sea
it dances, curl and roll, to fill
the shell whorls of my ears.

How can you lie forever lie like a marine
ha ha quick march left right left right right
out of the picture frozen shoes

A fierce tide of dreams, a monstrous engine driving through the
night, grumbling on and on in a rush of fever.
So much forgetting, each memory takes another shape,
becomes a story told by other men in other days, and nothing.
nothing stranger than this bed. From here I trundle like
an albatross, beating on air until it breaks from land; then
wheel, and soar away. And so I see the *Terror* and the *Erebus*
creeping through the bergs, weaving an aimless course among
the reflections of black cliffs, gliding into the hanging fog,
only the masts and topsails riding above the floss. Dead
men haul on sheets and buntlines, hoarse-voiced from rasping
air, hands bleeding onto snow white decks. And all around
on ice floes, splintered rocks, seals bark like mourning dogs.

East by North West by South full fathom five the bear's
up there it's snuffling I can smell hot hoary breath and
musty bones and dark fleas in its coat

My brother Tom says, said, that God's the Captain,
we must holystone the decks. Strange how I hear

his voice, his face a foreigner, yet I feel
his rough hand on my shoulder, neither warm nor cold.

He has a pair of hands had Tom, could splice and serve
so neat, but shy with girls and couldn't hold his beer.

Aurora Bor bazaars and Bethnell Green camphor and muslin
poor Tom boy on the deck cry wolf all darkness is
the source of light the bear the whitest bear

Another phantom of a dream stands out.
I heard a knocking on the door, rasp
of a jemmy on the coffin lid; a flood
of light that burst my head, a voice

that blew my temples wide, more voices
and a tapping on my chest. As if dropped

24

out of a womb I felt a stirring
as of life; cried out but they were deaf

it seems, and picked my pockets, probed
with knives and tweezers. I cried for darkness,
called on night - the awfulness of living
when its mask came off. I feared the warmth,

I trembled in the steaming bath of light, until
they hammered back the lid, let out the bright.

Cobwebs in cooking pots bones for glue stars
shaking quivering astral sea fat craw of Spring

Now that I've died that other death - now
I can hew the darkness with an axe,

break all the doors down, walk through
the river gardens and sleeping ships;

a hay meadow, brown nipples, snaking tongue.
Red redness of jaws strawberries and cream

Soft wind and the scent of islands, plums.
She rides bareback bare-breasted furry white

I know my strength. No wind can fail me now.
The bear is back and snuffling in the snow.

STRANGE FRUIT

Just now the music's
in the rain and in
the washing of the trees,
but when the light
fell on the roofs
and idle chimney-stacks,
it sounded like a band
of Irish pipes supported
by the wail of trains.

I would not wish to die
in such a breaking of a day,
on such a note,
but in the music of the rain,
now that's another thing,
with a score written
by those hands
that carved out flutes
and conjured fire. That
is the river that we run,
dance to be danced
deep in a forest
where the flowers thrust out
their genitals with greedy lips
and curl their phallic tongues,
or in the jig-sawn streets;
cadences of stone
arias of roots
and steel.

Music's a fine way
of seeing things, just as
a trumpet sounds like brass,
and violins become the voices
of bent pines, and drums
are rumbling stomachs

of wild beasts, palpitations
of fear-stricken hooves,
blues are the harvest
of the cotton fields.

Strange fruit,
mood indigo,
rain-wash on leaves,
a dying day,
chorus
of equinoctial geese,
a full moon drifts
behind a hanging tree.

DAVY JONES LOCKER

Down there, I tell you
it's cold silence, the living
few and mostly teeth.

Sometimes it only drizzles
a soft slow mud
forgetting light

Sometimes a battleship
comes gliding down, full
-manned and bleeding,

a liner, tramp, tanker
oozing like a squid, black
into black, its plume

expanding as it wreathes
the rigging
of a foundered brig.

And somewhere

Tom Danforth, ship's cook from Birkenhead,
half chinee, a muttering man but oyster eyed;
sometimes you'd have to poke his ribs to tell
he was alive. A face as round as a boiling coffer,
steaming and sweating in his stews, potages,

and god-knows-whats. He'd seven kids
in Hull, just six in Tiger bay. Last seen
hauling his duffle-bag aboard a whaler bound
for the Weddell Sea, to cool his fertile
bollocks, freeze him terminally.

Perhaps

Sly Comfitt, first mate
of the Penelope, no patience
with the sea, the winds
blew through him; a butler

or a cornet man washed down a river
like a fallen tree to wallow
adrift, barkless, gathering slime,
limpets, and by all accounts

colonies of biting crabs
from every continent. He had
no comfort in a bitter smile,
but nonetheless we missed

the rake of his thin shadow
on a sunlit sea, after we slid
him over the side wrapped in
an old sail, off Cape Harmony.

Surely

Lars Gregersen, foretopman, a Dane
from Jutland, gone to sea at twelve

and had no other mother than a wave,
no home except a cuddy hole. Some

forty years upon the sea, salt addled
cossetted by tarts in Valparaiso, Macao,

Lourenco Marques, piano bars in Oran.
A man who had a way with rope, whose

anvil hands could carve a magic ship
from ebony. A man aloft in a foul night

off Finisterre, tumbled from the yard
unnaturally, all silent like - you know
they mostly scream

MAPPA MUNDI

listen to the music
sound of chains
seed from Pharoah's tomb
rustling in bitter fields
listen to each note
each scream across
the hard distance whips
racks laughter
of children
on stinking heaps

        but there are angels
        there are hands
        white dawns even
        in still shadows and
        the scrape of pavements
        there are corners
        candles and the careful fire
        in iron grates
        some walking

        running through trees
        girders
        pickers of strange fruits
        tillers
        reapers
        butchers/lovers
        a beating of heads
        on winter
        desperate anchors

        a drawing of breath
        humming of the wheel
        steam
        angry smoke
        frantic copulation
        on a frieze around

the doomed temple
a casting of bones
antlers
brusque rub of shoulders
inward eyes
and clocks

In the pit of our breasts we are together,
in the heart's plantation we traverse
a summer of tigers

flame orchids
under the shadow
of creeping dust
winding its scales
about stubborn breasts
sleeping hips
while the harsh cries
of crickets echo
through forests
that died before
the first fierce penetration
among mountains
that sheltered
nursing sharks
before the gods
descended
before names

saliva trickles
from the jaws
of hills the blood
of dinosaurs is sealed
in rich red soil
feeding the herds
of angry apes
that fled the trees
to batten
on dew grass

forge sacred knives
grovel before temples
raised on piles
of bones

under the volcano
everywhere fire
and furnaces
the stolen flame
harnessed
to the crucible
gold wire
drawn about white
necks searching fingers
that spurt blood
from painted nails
to fall
on altars drenched
by wars where
golden calves
graze
among sunflowers

everywhere
flying ants
and strange infections
swarms
that seek no flowers
make bitter honey
everything that lives
has something eating it
so that the secret music
is drowned
by teeth

he that made the wheel
made crosses
hands that strung the harp
forged axes

32

uneasy waters
storms blind
silences
mouths with fins
drifters with hooks
tridents nets
moonrakers
ticks on the ocean's flanks
sea urchins
who only return to spawn
die gasping
among stones

there is still time
to pause beside the stream
kiss frozen lips
watch
evening pelicans
lying on the wind

JOCOTEPEC

Jocotepec (pronounced Hok-oh-tepeck) is a village at the western end of Lake Chapala, province of Jalisco, Mexico.

1.
the sun
has caught the mountain vultures
peer down where the village stirs
talking in its sleep, out on the lake
tired arms draw in tired
nets starveling fish

high noon dust
laid droop-headed
horses without strength
to flick the flies
around the square sleep sits
on worn shoulders heat
drowns all the shadows
on the land

from porticos the beat
from juke boxes groups
of mariachis twin speakers
in the church belfry drive
out the evil demons of the day
men wash out dust devils
with the juice of cacti
call on their gods
Carranza, Villa, Obregon,
Zapata, Juarez, Hidalgo, till
one by one and four by four
their shadows slip away to hide
and harbour in adobe

2.

Cold water, dawn water
on the ropes
and my hands, brother.
Haul, Pedro, on the net,
as I with the oars,
for fish, for silver
in the palm.
Pass me the gourd, Pedro,
the moon doesn't warm
like wine.
Haul away, Pedro,
for bread for our children
and a jug of mescal
at midday.
Haul up the sun, Pedrito,
in this net,
to warm my hands,
my heart.

3.

april opens its dry mouth begging
seedcorn restless in the bed so
hopeful maguey roots urgent in red soil
crickets beseeching the clouds
that gather over distant hills to lay
their waters on the land to father
bread tortillas flowers to cool the lips
of summer with the wine that flows
from the jaws of thunder

4.

Alicia with scrubbed face
dress hands complexion
of a race that lived
in the sun before the altars
ran with blood, before
the whips and crucifixes arrived
on the east wind scrubs

her life away to rear three
children by her man who fled
because he hadn't a woman's
courage to endure for all
his pride and pistols in the belt,
Alicia from an ancient line
born of agave and mesquite

5.
mist on the lake
the bus a stage the cast
an inconstant troupe
of vagrants wrapped
in rough cloaks and cotton,
the blind guitarist
weaving the warp and weft
a special magic joy
sorrow bite
of gyves shining silk
rainbows icy airs
melted snow blood
on bridal sheets
and shrouds, the precious
visions of unseeing eyes
that fill the bus
with all the scents
of morning songs
of plumed serpents

6
his widow gave me Armando's coat,
not the one with the tear
where the knife slipped
into his life but still familiar,
sometimes he wears it in my room,
for the rest it idles in the wardrobe
but every now and when I take
it out and walk and talk with him

7.
here the women
there the men the men
have hooves forever jinking
into some distance roping
white bulls riding in buses
with a suitcase tied
with string to cross dark borders
lost children sparring fighting
cocks mustangs while the women
wash and bake dig die
pour their nurturing
into the insatiable soil

8.
smell of ashes gunsmoke blood
round the ruined hacienda nettles
in corners of living rooms the dead
betrayed by the crying wind frogs
on the lips of the long-dry well

9.
fiesta
here they make horses dance
around the floats tinsel
macabre christs, apostles
with droop moustaches lips
strain on brass music
blown crystal sparkling
in the sun a company
of *rurales* ride black-eyed
on unshod ponies cloaks
of dust only their rifles
shine polished like coffin
handles streets filled
with candy penitents
vivas wondering children
fireworks all the torn

calendars of the year's
sorrowing forgotten

the music dies the lake
a virgin silver
clasped in the mountain's
iron arms

MANU

do you remember george
how quiet the river smooth
a sated snake its long
intestine rough
with undigested cedars
how butterflies gorged
on crimson meat
and how the canopy
had captured night
pinned it to earth spewed
from mouths
of ants and shining beetles
how the forest walls
shut out the cold
and steel and nations

a world we smell
in early morning dreams
lies still unborn
and everything that *lived*
was wise

ten days we drove
against the stream
ten nights we lay
and listened to the stars
and clouds that fought
among dead stones
and heard no other human voice
no drums
no preachers

we were the secret spies
of tribes that gathered
in the hills

with smoking guns
and whetstones

do you remember george
how quiet the river smooth
and the green walls
that breathed

ODERSFELT

DEER HILL

a vibration starts up, vague and insistent

The west wind's singing through the ling,
a curlew weeps its notes, the millstone grit
against my back bears scars
of masons' wedges, of the unnamed men,
scavengers of stone, weavers
of fleeces and salubrious dreams
who slaked the thirsts of hunger
with thin ale, the women racked,
bent, blinded at the wheel,
the childrens' fingers raw
and blistered.

And I happen to know that
the young blonde and brunette
in the Rose & Crown are discussing
the merits of the car ferry from Hull
or Dover if you're going to Belgium.
The old man in the corner moans
how things ain't what they were,
and that is the lie of it.

Deer Hill sleeps in the sun.
someone is renovating a weaver's cottage.
Interest rates are rising.
Kiwi fruit
is on offer at Tesco's.

In Odersfelt Godwin had six carucates of land for geld where
eight ploughs can be. Now the same has it of Ilbert but it is waste.

There's water dogs about,
they scurry over Buckstones Moss
and Garside Hey, licking

at Goat Hill, they course the sky
off on a run past Birchencliffe
and Ainley Top, a straggling pack
of grey-backed hounds without a voice
or whipper-in, but sure as hell,
as Billy Prest might say,
the wild horsemen of the rain
will follow as night falls
on day.

All through the wind shout
voices from the past, grey cottages,
grey chapels, ruined mills;
a hooter's morning moan,
crack of a bargeman's whip,
clatter of looms, whine
of wheels, hum of spindles,
serpent hiss of steam.

But just for now
shafts glint on the reservoir
at Blackmoorfoot and light
the catalogue of roofs
beside the valley of the Colne
right down past Cowlersley
and Paddock Brow
to Huddersfield. And Sextus Tupper
with his whippet, Quick,
are headed for the Warren House,
the new one that replaced the old
up on the moor, where William Horsfall,
on his horse, was felled
by the Luddite bullets of George Smith
and William Thorpe and died
the day after in the pub.
Quick has his special corner in the bar.

I asked of everything
if it had something more

something more than shape and form,
and so learned that nothing was empty -

A dog-day sweating under the sun, Quick
sniffs a morning turd donated by Caress,
Constance Enwright's dappled bitch, beside
the towpath of the narrow boat canal (disused).

Sextus pulls out his silver box to take
a pinch of snuff, snorts, sneezes, wipes
his nostrils with a bunch of flowers
imprinted on a handkerchief. The whippet

padding by his human's side, they tow
their images through those of trees, walls,
foxgloves and crouching fishermen and clouds
that loiter in the redundant water. Sextus

gets dreaming of cool frothing beer and counts
the pennies in his purse, then dreams again
of tomorrow and his pension cheque, the pub,
the butcher, then to cook pigs' livers

for Quick's weekly treat, an afternoon racing
in the betting shop, more beer, the chippy
and a choice of dominoes at the Liberal Club
or darts in The Wheel to lay the day away.

He day-dreams what he's trained to dream,
his other worlds are hoarded for the night,
when Quick will twitch, whimper in his sleep
and Deer Hill silver under a cautious moon.

Sadness. I need
your black wing.
So much sun, so much honey in the topaz,
each ray smiles
in the fields
and everything is light around me,
all an electric bee in the sky.

She's breasted the ramparts,
panted her way up Castle Hill to cool her lips
round a pint of bitter which
she shares, in an ashtray for Caress,
who stretches on the turf beneath
a bench and shaded from summer
by the folds of Constance Enwright's
flowered frock. They say that this
was once the fortress of a queen,
where Cartimandua reigned
(or was it Aldborough, by Boroughbridge?)
and anyway the lady and the bitch
are regal in their quiet content.

Connie takes out her backy box
and rolls herself a cigarette. Sucks
in the smoke, breathes out a fog
that's lazy in the stationary air.

The finger of the Emley mast
points to a passing jet, which
sweeps her off her feet and out
of now to a lost February package deal
to Benidorm; laughter of the bars,
the beach, but most the day she saw a sea
of almond blossoms, smelled their smoke.

Caress decides it's time to leave,
licks at the nearest flesh to paw.

Poetry is pure white.
It comes out of water wrapped up in drops,
it wrinkles, piles in heaps,
the skin of the planet must be stretched,
the sea's whiteness ironed;

Often the subjects of Sextus Tupper's dreams
are distant mountains plumed with clouds,
nursing deep sky-blue lakes within their folds

44

and creases swathed in conifers and green
as the sea-grass in a Cousteau film, bursting
with pine cones amber brown, shiny as a vixen s coat.
On other nights he might take off to the desert,
ride a roan mustang along the tracks of antelopes
between the pillars of red cliffs, his Springfield
rifle slung across his back, a wide sombrero,
boots and spurs, slitted eyes alert for smoke
and other Indian sign, or circling birds.

He likes the ones about steam trains he drives,
the white-winged ships he sails, but there are
those that make the sweat glands flow and some
so blue he doesn't dare tell them to the dog.

Everything was alive,
alive, alive, alive,
like a scarlet fish,
but time
with a rag and night
kept rubbing out
the fish and its heart-beat:

The mist is fired
with esoteric light,
fills the Colne valley foot,
from Crow Trees Road
to Spring Wood Hall,
as high one side
as Hazelgrove,
the other
to Scar Top.

By Lees Mill Farm
the air's so thick the world
becomes a catalogue
of sounds and smells;
clover and nettle,
magpie and bus, thud

of a football, shout
of a train. Water
has the mouldy scent
of death or lichen
on gravestones,
and boy and girl
and bird and dog
inhabit a white night.

The mist condenses
on the stones, the cars,
a horseshoe nailed
above a door,
on time itself,
on silent bells,
impatient hearse
abandoned font,
an anvil
in the breaker's yard

Above the mist
it's open sky,
sharp shadow,
mirror clean,
and purple
shot with granite grey
on the shoulders
of Deer Hill.

NEW STREET

has seasons,
times and tides,
and most of it
is not that new.

Just now
the surge isn't about,
the sun still

sulking somewhere
to the east of Hull,
though not as far
as Minsk
or Omsk;
the shops' eyes
closed, pavements
asleep, dustbins
waiting
for dustbin trucks,
the coldest
and most silent hour.

Things change

The walls
reflect
the early morning
beat
of feet and
the first bolts of sun
warm the breast
feathers
of pigeons perched
on pediments,
sparrows
on high
windowsills.

Things change

Ben Solomon turns
the corner, steps by
the Jug and Bottle, Stolen
from Ivor, Capolito,
Wots in Store, the Merrie
England Coffee Shop
without a glance, but
in an empty window next

to Next, sees his reflection,
grey on a background of white.

He stops at the entrance
of the arch that leads
to the Union Bank Restaurant
and Bar, notes the flood-tide
coming in from Cloth Hall Street,
Ramsden, all the yards
and ginnels, arcades, roads
that run into the New.

Joshua Umbabwe and Frankie Wells
loom up outside the front
of Marks and Sparks where once
was Thornton's Temperance Hotel.
They're on their way to sweep
the litter up along the bit
that used to be the Buxton Road.
This is the making of a day,
as Josh might say, that doesn't shake
the world but could be better if
the time was right and Town would
score the winning goal tonight.

Clicking her way on angry heels,
Candy O'Shea is less concerned
with football than her partner's
flagging dick and how
she'll find the money for
the baby's shoes and Council Tax,
puzzling how if and when she'll tell
her boss she doesn't fancy him
but still get Friday mornings off.

Buskers lay down their caps
at decent intervals, prams drive
a way through spin drift
of shoppers, students, reps,

etcetera, et al, and Bill
and Freda Beckenshaw.

Things change

Pigeons are pecking at the feet of Alfred Scarr
who's mouthing on a jumbo sausage roll, its flaky
pastry blown about and seized by beaks. Sparrows
hop here and there and flit from bench to bench, from
munching temps to masticating Town Hall clerks, and
some employed and un or past their sign-on dates.

The Jug and Bottle's filling up the guts of OAPS
with bitter, crisps and nuts, and reggae music
beats upon the ears through dreadlocks and Paisley
Jim thumps on the bar to get another half-an-half.
Mark's pulling pint on pint but still has in his head
the threads he's spinning for a short-story plot
he's working on on course for his degree and how to
structure it around the redhead in the window seat.

A sea of accents fills the bar, broad echoing vowels
of northern moors, hills, mills, mingle with those
of Glasgow, Caernavon, Islington and Crewe and
Kingston, Bridgetown, Port of Spain, Lahore
and Cork and all ale-whetted, blowing gusts of smoke.

Candy O'Shea's half listening to the grim story
of Tom Dickson's life or so it seems although
its subject is his visit to the DSS last week.
There's a great deal of holding forth on matters
of considerable import to bookies' clerks
and football gates and Tony Blair, the Queen,
the Pope, budding musicians and the Reverend Stokes
whose sermons concentrate on sex and dope.

Outside, a sudden hiss of rain drives window-shoppers
into shops but even so the patrons of the pub thin out.

Things change

The early afternoon is brisk
and bustles like a flock of pink
flamingos in a lake, leaf-cutter ants
or rabbits on the run. It's fair
to say that no one hears
the feet that passed here yesterday,
nor those of those who never heard
of tarmac or TV, who maybe even thought
the world was flat, the stars
were fixed and all roads led to Rome,
thunder and lightning battles
of their gods and lived and loved
and died without a credit card.

The Big Issue seller surely
has no thought of that
and certainly today
is not what was.

Things change

The sun drops
under Chapel Hill,
the day-stream
ebbs away. Tom Dickson's
off to catch
the 361
to Marsh whereas
his grandad used
to go by tram,
popped his clogs
in the battle of the Marne.

The shutters
and the grilles come down,
night sidles in,
New Street becomes
a silent sweep
of lamplight broken

50

by spasmodic bursts
of song and shout.
Nomadic groups
defy the silence
and police, seeking
from bar to bar
and club to club
some magic answer,
coupling of delight,
that's always promised
in some other place.

A hen party squanders
by Dolcis, Miss Selfridge,
Principles, Woolworths,
that face the window
of Worldwide Choice.
Squeals of laughter
shake the glass
of Our Price
and the Topman shop.
A half moon grins
in a silky sky.
Bob Clayburn says
that means more rain
but he's the one
that married Lilac Betts.

Things change

St GEORGE AND VARIOUS DRAGONS

This is St George's Square
not exactly
that is by no means
quadrilateral but I doubt
that wyvern whacker
would be worried
any more than pigeons

by its dimensions
though St Christopher (that was)
might feel aggrieved by its name
on account of the near continual
tide of travellers

there is a station

there are taxis

there are buses

there are people

an hotel

etcetera

a lion stalking
over a roof

and do you know insists Harvey Stubbs
that some nights in the month
at most particular hours and elevations
the moon shines through that lion's guts?

Harvey is careful
of his image
his pork-pie hat
tweed jacket jeans
green and purple trainers
he is notable

by his presence
as is the lion
and the absence
of wyverns

A great lion came from far away:
it was huge like a silence,
thirsty, hungry for blood,
and behind its posturing
it had fire like a house has,
it burned like a mountain of Osorno.

the lion
wanders through
a squall of rain,
prowling the kingdom
of his roof
stares down on
the migrant herds
that graze and roam
the square
and Harvey Stubbs
waiting
for the gates
of the Railway Tavern
to be unbarred

and you would be well advised
not to laugh at Harvey
and his fashions
he knows that death
is not an option
smiles
into his beer
and when he ambles
towards Northumberland Street
to cash his giro
winks at the king of beasts

It found only solitude
roared from uncertainty, from hunger –
the only thing to eat was air,
air the colour of birds,
unacceptable sustenance.

53

behind the elegant facade
of the station a train
disgorges and engorges
but Harvey Stubbs
is not apparent
not a trainspotter
or twitcher
or counter of pennies
and his liberality
extends and extends
given any fraction
of an opportunity
as does an imagination
more comprehensive
than the entire railway network
which is to say
he's just an ordinary bloke

Flo Stubbs is just after
coming from the Olde Hatte
and a chat & sup
steers a course
for the Head of Steam
to wait for Harvey on
his evening rounds
sits by a window
with a glass of red
and for no reason whatsoever
is filled with a torment
of unweathered joy
and even when
she spots her Harvey
under his pork-pie
still holds her lips
in a sensuous smile
even greets him with a nod
and doesn't bother to ignore
Barrabas Sykes
leering from the bar

54

Sad lion from another planet,
... with only an empty maw
some out-of-work claws
and a tail like a feather duster.

St. George according to tradition
was born in Palestine and martyred
at Lydda circa Ad 323 and there's no evidence
that he is related to Harvey Stubbs
who was born in Outlane circa AD 1948
is a brickie and his mother
was a martyr to arthritis
nor is there anything in the rumour
that he is descended from Jean Louis
Andre Theodore Gericault who painted
battles wrecks and the insane
though Barrabas Sykes could be

it is entirely possible
that Harvey is descended
from Robin Hood
as one grandmother
came from Barnsdale
and was a Fletcher

but there's no doubt
that Harvey Stubbs is related
by the trade of his hands
and head to men
who laid each block
of stone on stone
who raised
the station's columns
reared the Lion's Chambers
to the sky
carved the old king
of beasts
who smothered in the smog
is now replaced

by a fibre-casted
offspring or such-like
and Harvey likes to think
he hears it roar
the nights the storms
fall down upon the town
from Bolster Moor
and Scapegoat Hill

the symbols
of Flo's ancestry
are in strong hands
like those that milked
the scrawny cows that grazed
here when it was a field
it seems the generations will roll on
as Flo and Harve have raised their brood
of five two boys two girls and one
who hasn't yet made up its mind

The Head of Steam
is warming up
for Blues Night
and the instruments
creep in and take
their stand accompanied
by those who pluck
their strings or blow
or finger keys beat
messages on drums

Flo has a partiality
for blues taken
with G & T
or vodka on the rocks
while Harvey says it's better
with real ale that holds
the bitterness of life and magic
in the essence of its breath

the night rolls on
the air is beaten
by the 'Stormy Monday Blues'
'Cocaine' and 'Help Me'
'Let The Good Times Roll'
'Rock Me Baby' 'Mannish Boy'
'Crossroads' 'Sweet Home Chicago'
'Everyday I Have The Blues'

the clock ticks
on an empty face
the sad songs soothe
with heart-ease
patrons of the pub
entangled in a skein
of sound a world
that's shrunken
to this space

the music dies
glasses are gathered up
a spell is busted
time comes barging in

outside
the moon rides
on the lion's back
shines on the taxis
in their ranks
casts a lop-sided
and half-lidded eye
on the bricks and stone
of Odersfelt

FATHER TIME

He said he had lived in an age
of great horses,
and their soft lips would nuzzle
the back of his hand.
Golden plovers whistled in the mist
to land on the furrows
polished by rain.

Cottages sat like tea-cosies
round the dark beverage of poverty.
Scythes swished
while the reapers chewed
the stems of sorrel, and in Autumn
scavenged the rings of mushrooms
where cattle grazed
on the fog.

He said the meadows
were as old as his time;
their flowers the jewels
of all his children
and the food
of everlasting bees.

But though he had heard
the clatter of mowers
and the hum of thrashing-machines,
he had scarcely noticed
the long plumes
from tall chimneys down the valleys,
or entered the rooms of alchemists
and accountants,
and now he must rummage
for a spray of buttercups
to lay on a lover's grave.

HELL OR HIGH WATER

*The people in the Golden Hinde saw the Squirrel almost
swamped by a huge wave. She rose again, and immediately
afterwards Sir Humphrey was observed by those in the Hinde
seated in the stern with a book in his hand. They heard him
call out,* "Courage my lads. We are as near Heaven by sea as
by land," *and that was the last ever seen or heard of the
gallant knight on this earth.*

A wave came roaring out of a hollow sea,
and in the still curve of its lips
the very scent of putrefaction.
Not all its salt, not all its sound
had any part of life. It had a full bosom
of whale's milk, squid's beak, an oyster's
grey green skin, and carried like a bouquet
in its hair the masts and spars of broken ships.
It was cold, angry, surfeited, wild
with moon madness and the pain of age,
and the unfathomable guilt that builds the pearl.

NUNC DIMITTIS

When the sea hog leaps
sharp watches keep.

We were close off the Cape of Finisterre
and the dolphins were dipping as far as perceptible
and a kind of anger was fastened in the sea.

That night took Ben Arden and there was no way
to go back for him. It was when all those fishes
were leaping and blowing from rise to set

and the moon near out, that I saw this green island
to the West, where no island was, and it was
like a place you would dream to die - that evening

of the night that drowned Ben Arden in a westerly gale.
Look there, girl, look, look there beyond the pier.
Is that an island where no island ought to be?

TEMPER OF STEEL

A coral world
skeletons of words, pines,
kisses, webs, a blind altar
to a god who hides
in the milk of genitals,
in the red ocean of the dead,
rises clear, cold, to run
through weeping hills to prophecy
in markets, build mountains
from groans, wrecked ships, aspens;
concertos that echo
across glaciers, fill tombs
with white music of orchids.

The seed becomes the fruit,
the fruit the seed, the dead
he living, for a while,

a while.

When the wind comes running,
seas break among columbines
and eggs of avocets lie in cold nests,
merchants and ministers mount the four horses,
songs of innocence are smothered in velveteen,
where the voices to defy gardens?
What's the temper of your steel?

When the gold masks are torn
from skulls, when slugs are sacred,
the brown rat restored, apples
vindicated, crows and snakes absolved,
then, will graves open their doors
to thrushes? Will the blind worm sing?

THE ROAD TO DAMASCUS

All along Jensen Avenue poverty had spilled
out of the houses, even the dogs and cats
had caught it and a harsh and sulphurous light
had faded the T-shirts of the jobless welders
and the blouses of their pubescent daughters.

The newsagents on the north-west corner
didn't sell wallets and the glass case
full of pens and watches was sealed
with a patina of dead dust. That's not
to say that dignity had been abolished,

nor that the music that inhabits aspirations
was silenced nor the drums of passion dismantled.
Children blew about the street like crisp packets,
doorways were carpeted with condoms, laughter
fell about, half an hour after the bars opened.

It was while he was stealing a girl's bicycle
from the alley by the chapel that Amos Dupre
caught sight of a fluorescent angel lurking
behind the tombstone of Andrea Bellini, mother
of Patsy Fate and a seven piece rock band.

And it told him to get his thieving hands
off the bike and pointed out to him
that in Draper's Close a fish-merchant
had just parked a Ford Capri and neglected
to remove the keys from the ignition.

THE PIEMAN

It was plain to see through the glass
that the country moving behind it was flat.
The sky had a grey face and,
because trees and hedges weren't disturbed,
it seemed generous despite pylons
trailing their cables, and being spiked
by arrogant and pitiful steeples.

He was sure that beyond the petulance
of the argument between track and train,
the young corn, the blackthorns
and rehearsing birds out there
weren't at all happy - could be
they were angry with this
cold of Spring and its lack of conformity
with the reminiscences of alders.

This speculation reminded him
of prisons
and leg-weary foxes,
culled kangaroos,
sudden widows, blue rosettes.
He decided this sky was a sea
surging over cemeteries
with the silence of tiles.

He became grateful
to the ticket-collector,
the trolley of sandwiches
and refreshments and black shining
hair of the girl opposite,
who licked her red lips
and smiled into the face
of a magazine called WOMAN.

THE PHILOSOPHER

He sat beside the stream and saw
time passing; over it there flew
a swarm of gnats, some mayflies
paused, copulated, died to feed
trout that swam the tide of rain
that lately rode the clouds
coagulated in a lazy sky.

He sat, a lonely figure in a bar,
watching how hours became the smoke
of roll-ups drifting in the faces
of Albert Einstein and Thelonius Monk
staring from black varnished frames,
framed by Bill Bartlett for five quid,
manufactured in his boss's time.

Settled in the easiest chair he watched
the box to see how tiger sharks were born,
the age it took for stalactites to mate
with stalagmites if separated by eons
of dripping tears from roof to floor
of a deep cavern far below a sky haunted
by ghosts of blue and crimson moths.

He heard the roaring of the sun, the sea
that ground the granite into sand.

THE THEORY OF CHAOS

As Shakespeare said, Charlie not Bill,
there is a time in the affair
when you must get the fuck out.

Ted Shanks, a dreamer remarked on
June Wilde's walk and its after effect
on those in long trousers, even skirts.

Neither has much regard for Carl Bugatti
and his mouth organ, but obsequiously agree
with his wife in her selection of dentures.

Not one of all those four has heard
of Dandy Jim Davidson who resides noisily
in Ossett with some goats and a collection

of erotic cockroaches, but his altercation
with Black Toby over the existence of quarks
caused a circling of ripples still undetected
by seismologists and the perseverance of dowsers.

No. 18 TAYLOR STREET

The window opens
to the pitch of grey slate
and only half a sky.
I have no jealousy
of vistas and houses
that boast panoramas,
court exclamations.

The trees have no eyes,
the mountain
isn't dazzled.

My lease is temporary
and grey is the colour
of the dustman's cap.
If I'm not here,
off to visit a friend
or some distorted memory,
an imagined canyon,
or just dead
the slates on each roof
will remain. Each morning
lights appear
in mysterious windows,
doors open and bang shut,
pizzas and children
will be delivered,
and even here
birds bathe
in the gutters.

What is left of the sky
is ample.

THE MAN WITH NO NAME

I asked him
where he came from.
He said:

I come from my mother's waters,
from my father's well,
come grimed with brick-dust,
stained by my brothers' blood,
scorned by accountants,
washed in sweat.

Horses see the dust of my passing,
snort their impatience.
Crows watch my shadow,
are familiar,
worms sense my steps
and are expectant

My inheritance is clay,
and offal from sumptuous kitchens.
I'm a conjuror of fishes.
My nostrils know the language
of faithless streets,
effluvium of mines.
I pass from farm to forge,
from mill to ship
and each one steals
the droplets of my sweat,
my hours, my loves
and no one calls
my name.

I asked him
where he lived
but he was lost in the crowd.

HE SAID THERE'S NOTHING

concentrates the mind
like a health inspector.

I said wolves.

He said what wolves.

Wolves I said concentrate
the mind wonderfully,
it's something in the howl.

He said gibberish.

No, wolves.

Gladys, he called
the length of the bar,
don't serve this one
any more.

THE WATERSPOUT

The turning of an Archimedes screw
sucks water from its heaving up to where
water drifts waiting in a sombre cloud,
waiting to fall as water in a drift of rain,

like leaves that drop in autumn to the soil
to rot among the roots that ravish them
to spread a canopy that sucks the sun
until the turning of the globe calls in

the nights that harbour frost, an alchemy
transmuting green to gold before the white
of snow lays on its eider down and crows,
their darkness like the mouth of death,

like water deep below the eye of sun, like
a black hole and its relentless screw, wait
for the nights to shrink and leaves to spring
and dress the branches where to build a nest,

their shadows on the winter wasted fields
transient as wakes of old and desperate ships.

ATLANTIS

they know it's there
    I know, the trouble
is
  they keep moving
it around
      inching it
past
each generation's wall
    of knowledge, bricks
of straw and mud
soft
as the ocean's
detritus the roofs
    always two fathoms
below the diver's
aspiration
    always beyond
the next field
of kelp

NODDING OFF

there came a whisper
in the grass
your life is lived
your dying
soon be done

he didn't shout
or say a prayer
just looked
in the mirror of a lake
smelled the moss
took a pinch of soil
to feel
its soft endurance
sat on a rock
listening
for the slap of waves
to lull him
into all of time to sleep

DANSE MACABRE

All past the dancing days, all but
their drifted sounds and scents
plucked from a wind that's been far
travelling along its reckless paths
and sometimes sings, sighs, roars,
comes with a mouthful of spit
among the pines that lean
over water troubled by a moon.
Time mists the windows of the eyes
that search within the basket
of the skull where sensuous whispers
of such loves that had no fear
combine, a sad chorus in each dawn
now that the dancing days are done.

SUPPOSING

I guess the time has nearly gone
for battling with pints and lust
lies low as a wounded fox,
not like
the loot Prometheus stole,
not like
the fierceness of a day
shiny as a guardsman's boots.

I guess the time has nearly come
to finger pages of worn books,
compose a score of willows' tunes,
scramble
for sapphires in the slag,
harrow
the soil for planting
winter wheat

HELL FOR LEATHER

He found the brown shoes on the verge
beside the Rochdale Road up on the moor.

Who'd dump a pair of shoes there with no feet?
A sailor from Lithuania? Plumber outward bound
for Blackpool for an august week? A lover
looking for another half? A drunken shepherd
on a spree? A hard man on his way to death?

Shoes bear the scars of life, their soles
know all the ginnels, cobbles, grass, the mud,
rugs, lino, pavements, slime that clasps the rain,
so many paces in the hunt, the chase that pumps
the heart, slow step of sorrow, stamp of hate,
march of arrogance, stumble of blind faith.

A crow lumbered by, a curlew trilled. He took
the shoes home, chucked them in the bin.

A PARTRIDGE IN A PEAR TREE

Catching a swordfish in a parallax,
that is to say in leaping from a wave
it seemed to hang forever in the air,
is consonant with how my uncle Fred
appears in church, or smelling roses
in a chippy, how wigwams would sit
in Barnsley or on Queen's Parade.
But then the moon is still up there
in hours belonging to the sun. Time
has its own displacements, some believe
they constantly recur themselves, once
Cleopatra or Euripides to reappear
as Joan of Arc or Kublal Khan. One day
I swore I saw a poet in a hardware store.
But miracles are forged by will and time
creates a parallax when time stands still.

ODE TO THE ANNOUNCEMENTS OF SPRING

This morning I decided to be old,
sink into a luxurious decline,
lie back, upholstered, sprawl out,
recline on a velvet cushioned ottoman,
only take the air when thermals twist
above the harvest fields, drink wine
from grapes that suckled on the sun
before a fire fed with scented pine,
cap the night with brandy in a glass
that catches flames to samba round
the orbit of its bulging curves.

But then a cuckoo cooed and bragged
and I was young again, sad, mad and bad.

MEMORY

your skin shines
silver in the night
I can feel
the moist hollow
of your knee
remember
how we made love
to celebrate
the dawn

memory is desire
satisfied
don't forget
our meeting

THE GREAT RIVER

we sailed in on the breath
of Africa
into the crimson scent
of shadows
and the lamps were lit
in Sanlucar
de Barrameda

we rode the tide
drawn by a crescent moon
to mountains
to a gypsy song
torn from the throat
of history
            the caravel
laden with bloodstained gold
for Santiago in the name
of the Most High King

we steered through mist
to the deep song
of black water
steered
for the golden tower
on the sweep
of the great river
Guadaquivir

78

INTIMACIES OF MORTALITY

stars release the energy of a million h bombs a second
said the telly and the doors of perception opened wide
for gordon witherness so he reached for another glass
of glenfiddich with the intention of closing them fast
before any more visions of the immensity of it all loomed
revealing the insignificance of even the olympic gods
and that of harry cope the landlord of the saracens head

last friday it had rained on the parade organised sic
by jason beryl broome illustrating poads bottoms place
in history over three thousand years and the bronze age
tribesmen celts romans angles et al pursued by a succession
of mediaeval stuart georgian fashions and uniforms etc
represenited the chaos of the past and celestial galaxies
when all the colours ran into each other and the gutters

this was a powerful parable of something he couldnt recall
bugger the ministries of transport agriculture n fisheries
mused gordon there is scarce time for the distractioins of
leaves and the mortification of countless hooved beasts
when all the philosophies are so essentially inadequate
and although gravity has converted polytheism to monotheism
it cannot be denied even by a pope that black holes suck

een while harry cope was polishing the glasses gordons eye
was caught in the web of lace across julie denims breasts
and he remembered his callow youth in several cowsheds
causing the desolation of his life to fall on him heavily
so that even a double 12 yr old malt couldnt cheer him and it
came to him that the collapse of the entire universe was
coming and real power lay in the satchels of bookmakers

jim holdbeck was locked up again last night said harry cope for
pissing on the statue of harold wilson this time not on
the bard in the foyer of the theatre when waiting for godot
was performed jim is as thick as a stipendary magistrate

responded gordon though probably smarter than shakespeare
or harold wilson for that matter if you consider it deeply
but after this one im off out to search the sky for comets

be extra careful where you make water abjured the landlord
which gordon witherness considered as good advice as any
certainly as solid as the prognostications of jude the opaque
or the greyhound selections of fast track jenkins or promises
of ada coldshaw the day before the arrival of her dole cheque
but doom was still in the air as he peered into the night and
saw not even a shooting star never mind a comets tail

one of these days or darks thought gordon i shall implode
into my own magnificence then explode in a shower of sparks
and went on his way with unconstipated alacrity singing in a
fruity voice a number of snatches of psalms my funny
valentine followed by a scatalogical rendering of god save
the fucking queen so that the shadows fled the sombre corners
of his heart and poads bottom shined in a sickly orange light

CONJECTURES ON AGING AND EVANGELISM

we ll gather lilacs in the spring again but that
thought gordon witherness isnt a rewarding pastime
for springs no better n worse than bloody summer
as cold as bloody autumn and as for bloody lilacs
they should be left on bloody bushes where they belong

the years had accumulated on him as muck in a midden
that he couldnt be bothered to shovel out had left
a plethora of sour and revolting tastes in his gorge
remember the alamo he proposed or pately bridge why
do the monks no longer monk at fountains or rievaulx

where are the knights templar and the fearless disciples
of jacob crunch where the guardians of the relics of fred
the eulogists of eisenbacker and the opaque chameleons
is the voice of the dotterel still recorded in the wapentake
of nether thriddings do the ghosts of doncaster smoke cigars

this surely was a monday to beat all mondays muttered gordon
playing a fugue on his tin whistle but the saracens head
will open up in half an hour he estimated maybe harry cope
may know if the brotherhood of greengrocers and arkwrights
still meet in the tabernacle of the holy remains of saint wix

the saracens head drew him though the landlord knew nothing
of the doings of the brothers but then cheered gordon up
with a fable of the drunken carpenter and the busker plus
the doings of ada coldshaw and the five sons of red fyber
himself the son of a cardinal and a big-titted milkmaid

a shaft of sun struck harrys nose and lighted up the bar
gordon slid three pints down which drowned the creeps
that churned his stomach drove out the blues until a grin
crept round his stubborn mouth eyes shone bright as brandy
the pub became the kind of place yd even take yr daughter

but then he didnt have one only a small sad dog whose
pedigree invited research and manners fervent execrations
the thing is remarked gordon my intensive studies of taoism
and research into the origin of looms have cast little light
on the vagaries of fortune and ramblings of jim holdbeck

but if the licensing laws were to be emended favourably
the amount of cerebral energy generated per extra hour
would in the same way that a monkey could write the bible
increase the possibilities of revealing the most secret secrets
showing the ultimate truths to be ultimately true

i couldnt agree more said harry cope id bet a tenner on it

SCENTS AND SENSITIVITY

been considering death a lot lately said gordon witherness
especialty since ava godfrey beat me at darts and dennis
culthorpe collapsed into his own septic tank last saturday
and still stinks he always did anyway responded harry cope
death has no problems for me its just a sleep you dont wake
from with a furred mouth and a headache but what if its like

a foreskin hiding another universe protested gordon or maybe
oberon harper is correct in his diagnosis of contagious
eternities fuck that for a start bellowed harry that wd be
too bloody much and went back to polishing glasses n ashtrays
theres some things best left to the imagination i ll drink
to that harry fill it up and dont dare offer a clean glass

like they do everywhere nowadays have you seen those leeks
in tony buckstones allotment bigger than bulls pricks even
his marrows are as fat as trucks what the hell is he using
probably starling droppings from the churchyard this time
could be gordon considering he was disqualified from the show
last year when his aubergines smelled of smoked anchovies

n horse shit thank heavens im not a gardener harry it wd
drive me to drink or bore me to death speaking of death
they buried the remains of bert fulkes yesterday not that
there was much to put in after hed been through glen ashbys
combine he could only be identified by two betting slips
which just goes to show mortality can be seriously serious

dont get yr yfronts in a twist gordon it may never happen

THE SOUND AND THE FURY

No tenderness for my son, nor piety
To my old father, nor the wedded love
That should have comforted Penelope

Could conquer in me the restless itch to rove
And rummage through the world exploring it,
All human worth and wickedness to prove.

> Dante. Divine Comedy. From version by Dorothy L Sayers.

He came out of that field, closed that gate. The moon
  had halitosis,
the sea tumbled while a bird that skimmed its ups
  and downs
piped to the echo of a departed wind. A drunken ship,
  sails slatting
on the buntlines at each roll, wallowed and groaned and
  farted
in the swells. The rudder had no grip, the helmsman's
  will was not
enough to hold the bowsprit levelled at a star. And when
  day slid up
behind land, it had the colours of used winding sheets,
  winked a red eye.

But you could say it wasn't quite like that, could say
  the field
was a metaphor for a large forest, no longer in its youth,
  the gate,
well, the gate was an open book. And all the rest was only
  smoke and glow
of a camp-fire under a conspicuous conifer that mountains
  had spared
and the stiff colours of winding sheets, not mentioned
  by shepherds
and meteorologists, by their nature have a relevance
  to lilies.

It could be that he swam into her eyes and that her lips
   were salted
and her skin - oh yes, her skin would silver like a river,
   flow all
about him, her hair wind with supple scents, wrap him
   in a time
of sand and cheap hotels that creak all night and are
   more anxious
than February buds; her love-bites blazoned on his chest
   like shields,
or runes scribed on a parchment in a time of centaurs
   and flamingo gods.

You see these things are always what they are and hold
   the night sounds,
tear the clapper from the bell, fill the wine men's cups
   with burgundy
to toast the brides and those not dead and bakers rolling
   out the bread
for those who shiver in the street. You hear the dark
   has many wings,
several ensembles and string quartets that lull toucans
   on their roosts
and humming birds that weave their nests in branches of
   Macrolobium trees.

Swifts smell the fingers of frost, bend their scimitars
   towards
a southern cross. The clouds they form pass fleetingly
   over the narrows
of Tarifa, leaving Mons Calpe well to port but break
   and scatter
in Morocco. They are the cumuli of dark, notes of autumn
   from a Viking score,
a fiddler's fancy in a Wicklow bar, but for the rest
   it means no more
than Sanskrit to a golf club bore or coppers to a dosser
   in the strand.

It's time the earth should steady up. It's hardly right
the geese
should have to drive so far and fast to breed when we can
do it
in the park. And more, we have our turbos in the skull,
altimeters
in the cranium; a clock with deadly hands, credulous
astrologers,
bus passes to crematoriums, tickets for an opening night
of Lovers' Paradise.
The moving finger dips into the till, pockets a three
dollar bill.

Surf breaks on a wounded shore while lightning shivers
like a sword;
hours drip from taps, off-licences and pet shops chain
their doors.
The streets behave like evening, surgeons lay down
their knives,
dogs doze in doorways and the open mouths of bars
begin to shout.
An alley leads down to a field, a gate and cliff-path
to that beach.
The ship sobers up, bows pointing at a star, and Ulysses
sails home to Ithaca.

PILTDOWN MAN

THERE'S SOMETHING ABOUT A WALL

He looked out of the window to see just a little sky
but mostly the trees' new leaves consuming all the horizons.
He looked at the wall; behind it and before it
staccato reflections of the man he was and was becoming.

Perspectives changed by perspectives;
moonflowers became sunflowers, white egrets pugnacious crows,
while the satin sounds that ships make with waves
rasped in the thin air to the clamour of fractious monkeys.

And in the caves where dancers twirled
to the ancient strings,
where men crawled like slugs in times of great rains,
round feeble fires,
gods were created, debated,
exiled to run to distant mountains, hide
in grim cloisters and spiked minarets,
with their retinues of maggots
and jackals; their gentle hands, angry mouths.

The wall being that door
holding all wisdom belonging to sleep and death,
laughter shining in the eyes of mice.
The wall pulsing like the ocean, blowing back and forth,
opening, closing when time leaped in and out
like a calendar, breath of an oyster.

Then in the window, not the wall,
the light fiercened by a star of blazing sun
- a glance of it - a greying of the pulse of day;
pendulum, sand, shadows' lengthening of stone,
autumn flight of teal, lamina of shale,
fish sleeping inside rocks.

Back to the wall, its obdurate transparency
  - a smudge of smoke no more alone
on this or any sea - night buses,
cautious trains, Columbus with leprous hands, you, me,
  - don't knock the bastard until you've searched
what you might be; moth, human nearly dog.

Brick on brick, stone on stone, the river's
muttering erosion to mud, stone, bricks, clay, teacups;
gargoyles spouting the liturgies of the beast,
man in ermine with a gore-stained pestle
grinding perfumes for a silky bed.

He took a nail, divided the wall;
its length, its breadth,
gripped the haft of a claw-hammer,
drove the iron into the vent of its hook.
The picture he'd chosen blue, but for a solitary bird;
nameless bird in the sea of the sky;
sweat rising to the sun, but not yet clouds,
not the smoke of its inheritance.

And he went down tide-green steps
that smelled of murder and pulpits, walking
on water until it closed over; his long hair
waving in the stream, clutching at tiny shrimps,
prawns that wheeled round
the boulder of his head;
his body hardened in the ooze, compacted under
the weight of heaven.

But he was undecided, considering
the colour, texture of the wall
in relation to the blue and the bird. Thinking
  - maybe the roses or a hay wain;
a snap of Torbay, or Alice in her pink dress - torn
between one or another - perhaps the grey horses;
the ploughman leaning

into the red soil, rolled up sleeves,
one foot in the stubble, one in the furrow;
a scavenging of gulls for evicted worms;
new-leafed elms, a dead oak for its eccentricities;
and yes, the nameless bird, left of frame,
to the right of the crooked steeple.

He decided that red was sharp,
pink had the strangest scents, blue the colour
of certain mountains; green and grey were ambiguous.

So he took the claw
of the hammer to the hook;
drew the nail from the wall; put his palms
against the smoothness - skin to skin –
peered into the hole that had been
the nail; into the vortex of its depths;
like a mole, a hawk in mist

The dew's smoke ran away; shadows strolled off
as quiet as elephants. He felt the vibrations
of termites, drumming of beetles;
drew a circle in sand with his finger;
watched the tide eat it, but came to no conclusions.

He'd forgotten his name,
all names, and was comforted;
went to sleep in the shade of something, dreamed
of something else, woke to another; grinned at them all
and all their pulsing echoes - boom, boom, boom.

MORNING GLORY

A rising exuberance came out of nowhere,
the morning quiet.
Newspapers were full
of personalities and massacres,
fat astrologers, gaunt politicians.

Out of the doom came sunrises
with ardent prisms; the scent
of chocolate, a murmuration of insects.
He started a frivolous debate
in an acropolis crowded with heavy gods and saints,
wafting a purple handkerchief under his nose
against the odours of gangrenous wounds;
shaking a finger at their excuses,
taunting them with infidelities.

Dismissing them to their quarters,
he steered for a lonely island;
dug up some clay,
toyed with it a while.
He manufactured many shapes and sizes,
breathed into them pious emotions;
but they ended up eating and killing
each other; filling the wind with dirges,
catechisms,. speeches.

So he went into the garden
among the erect satyrs,
dissolute and lascivious nymphs,
sixty-nine varieties of mandrake and a lotus border;
hunkered under a yew tree
playing poker with the children of Diogenes Freud.

OVENS AND DOCKS

The clouds exhausted,
gardens became peopled,
heads down, tails up,
tying labels to shrubs, filling
ovens with docks and dandelions;
repelling snails and aphids
and dark things that roam
beyond hedges.

She stood beside him at the window.
The ocean roared, and the break
of her hair was filled with sun;
her calm that of water's sheened surfaces,
her strength that of the long waves' rolling
under brazen skies.

She was all foam and the silence
that fills the hollows of undulations.

In Boca Raton there was a sea
like that; fleeced with sails.
Out of it came a wind
that blew the roofs off all the houses,
from Pozo Escondido to Los Campos de Lagrimas.

APERITIF

In Absolom's Bar and Cafe they were discussing
nignogs and several lost empires. And his pale skin
turned black; while the jukebox drummed out
the rhythm of chains. Old mills
were rebuilt; there was a flashing of watches;
tweeds had the patterns of bones. The thought
of dying gained in tolerance. But he recalled

her stern courage and smile like a dipping gull; so
the hunch of his shoulders shook out like a sail
to a surprising wind. And all the distances
called to him in familiar voices.

CONSIDERING

my cracked jaw
and lack of prehensile tail,
he thought:
I get by.
No more,
no less than many billions;
no less than the wind
unaware of its name
and implications.

And so far
I've not been raped,
burgled to any extent;
and murder
sits in corners.

Let me sleep
in the blanket of insignificance.

Neither the oak
nor the bee
has any useful answers.

HE THOUGHT, PERHAPS

it's all downhill from here;
this instant piled on instances,
mountain of rotten branches,
dead time, embraces, suck
of gravity.

He thought of laughter
in a brittle night; the cradle
beckoning, the grave somewhere,
here, there; a bird
opening its eyes to shout
defiance at the sun.

And where all water runs,
there shall be found
the past and future answers,
in a sea that closes
all the wounds of keels.

That's it, he thought,
as neat as apple pie.

OUTRAGEOUS BIRDS

The bed nursed him. When he closed his eyes
light poured in, and he found himself
in a desert broken up by smooth-skinned trees;
leafless but flecked by purple flowers.
The wind had lost its voices; branches
pale and patient, with a poor memory for rain;
roots writhing in cracked soil.
And nowhere he had known was more beautiful,
nowhere more cruel. So he steeled himself
against sleep, stretched out in the net of shade,
dreaming his daylit dream among white bones.

And it was the smallest birds
that shouted loudest; drilled the air
with stabbing tongues; until
he called back the night to silence them,
and, as far as is known, slept.

FLAMBOROUGH HEAD

sea fret
smoking rocks
ships' bells
ring down
the tides

in the white silence
long ships galleys
galleasses
cogs nefs hoys
schooners cutters luggers
hermaphrodite brigs
brigantines
barques pinks
chasse-maries
snows
ketches barquentines
colliers whalers
alum sloops and men-
o-war caught
in the whirlpool
of the mist

cries of desperate men
thunder of *Serapis*
Bonhomme Richard's guns
boatswains' piping screams
of boys drowned
curses squealing blocks
clank of capstans
wind sough and leadsmen
calling in the chains

a collier brig
uneasy
on the swell

the captain widening
his nostrils to the fog
breathes in the deadly
scent of land
hiding fear under
a blanket woven
by storms dark reefs
and snaking sands

the cabin boy
too young to know
the menace in the grim
silence scurries
about the deck
                    eyes
black water sky that's climbed
down ratlines
to the futtock shrouds
runs forrard under dripping yards
and stays to watch
the dolphin striker carve
the sea how the sea
fastens on the hull
how the hull answers
to the sea

fog lifts
from the cliffs
sun sparklIng
all the bells are gone

SIMONE STYLITES

Yes, it's my father over there;
that thin and horny man.
That's him
two miles to the East,
an ant on a reed growing through
the desert 's shimmering.

A blessed eremite ...
don't make me choke,

they come at sunset on their knees,
wrapped up in modesty.
But in the fall of night strip off
eight veils, arch back and open up
to moonbeams on their breasts,
shine them at the gaunt old goat
up on his pile. And down he peers
with watery eyes, slobbering,
gibbering on his pole; shins down
to peck among the ripened fruit.

My mother knew him when his skin was smooth; so
maddened him he dived from his cock roost into her satin,
creamed intimacies. They say it took six Libyans, a camel
and some borrowed oars to get him back up to the sky.

I've squatted here since puberty, two cubits higher
than my father's phallic pile, just high enough
to override the stench that mounts and trots downwind
from his shit-slavered pinnacle. Paradise is green,
Odin's halls steamy with mulled mead. Here dust dances
a dervish dalliance, whispering in the wings.
This theatre has only echoes, laughter of the dead,
rattling bones of dry voluptuaries, pious observances
of putrid bishops; winds full of ash, torn parchments
of bibles; the sun weighs like a coronet of lead,

and you could fry a lizard on the rocks. Days are penance
for the nights - the nights I slip down into cooled sand
and lionesses come to stretch their furs under the white hole
of the moon. And there I lie, my back against their dugs,
breathing the embers of their breath rank with hot entrails
of antelopes, gazelles. My breasts harden, bloom and swell.

That dry old stick
to windward,
blinded by arrogance,
frieze dried
and muttering prayers
to his imagined,
outraged God,
has no conception
how his seed filled,
flushed
with the first cream,
defied his starved angles,
drew its curves
out of the dunes' sweep,
crook of thighs, twist
of fingers in a suppliant sigh.

A camel train, wisp in sand-sky, crawls off;
the camels' lips disdainful, Berbers' eyes hawk-hooded,
blue as gun barrels, all grim veiled. All wind swept
as the dune ant's trail. All faces blurred to clean. All
time congested in a donkey's turd.

Back of beyond a mirage of the sea
with bustling sails and plumes
of blowing whales, islands
with green caves and almond trees; a city
scavenged by besotted dogs, its maze unkempt
with listing balconies, its cake shops
with half-moons of tangerines swimming
in a foam of cream, cool bars,
deep voices of guitars.

This my manna, this
and the sour smell of hares,
snails' slime and musk of bears, whipped
with the pinions of a partridge wing, flamed
with the evening's blazing, thrust
through budded lips.

Hear this -

Here this high summer
writ in evening
light.
Here this
an abstinence,
something taught,
something as taut
as teaching
a poor elephant
to smile.
This tall script
writ slanting,
summer height.
This obelisk,
summit,
ego
sum.

This and the pad of lions in the night

BAT WOMAN

HANGING IN

The child's crying woke her, so
she opened it a breast;
while the sky's slow turning
gave a comforting illusion of green corn,
golden harvesting, and the pulse
of migrating finches.

She attended to the drip of water
and remembered lovers;
each a tear,
with the taste of milk and aloes.

The child gurgled;
and the gutters.
They all fell asleep.

While they slept
dustmen were sweeping up
bird droppings and burger baskets.
So they woke
to a clean street, and rain
dropped through the wind
leaving some semblance of clarity, some
gloss of order. Bankers
stepped out on clicking heels,
umbrellas defending them
against the importunities of hunger,
no longer recalling the taste of milk.

The child whimpered against her fur.
She hugged it between the membranes of her wings,
shielding it from the terror of light,
dreaming her dream of long shadows,
a sky full of moths.

DOWNSIDE UP

I hang silent
in the cave.
An arrow shaft
lights on the paintings;
spears the dead herds
and charcoaled hunters.

Where are my sisters?
Mothers?

Not here
but in the litter of the floor,
afterbirth feeding the continuance of rats.
And there below
I see white thighbones,
skulls.

In this still air
I hear the wash of wings,
cries of unopened eyes, hiss
of vipers;
sniff the steam of blood.

There a grim moon
drops through a sea of pines.

But laughter's somewhere
in the pile;
arch of passion,
suction of desire;

the lift,
the thrust,
the gasp,
the smile.

FREE FALLING

Does he remember
Darkstone Copse?
Sunset dancing
to a south wind.

The almost touch;
the nearer drawing turns;
in and away,
away and in.
Sweat in the palm
against the partner's waist;
one, two and three,
the pipistrella waltz.

Skin rustle,
pungent glands;
pull lips
and genitals.
One red-eyed star.

Will he know the child?

AERIAL COMBAT

Proud fathers with sharp spurs
and hooded eyes;
defenders cf the faith -
patronage.
While we
who bear
the scars and suckle them,
they flatter
for our wedding gifts.

But we have wings,
the air, the night,
long memories;

tooth and claw.

GRAVITATION

She probed the dark for its echoes,
stroking the velvet curtain with her tongue.
It was full of wide acres
and the nightjar's trill; tread
of the moon's shadow over frosted fields.

We have no provenance, she thought, only
embraces, needles, shawls, the cup
of the bra; a pallet filled with straw,
stained with sweat and semen. Somewhere
the tide sweeps clean,
stilts stalk the ooze;
there are fish with crimson scales, winds
heavy with honey and the quetzal preens his wings.

She swung round Hardburn Close;
free-wheeling, swinging hips; feeling
her body, not its weight. Freeing
the sour scents, making distance dance.

She laughed and dived into a swarm of gnats.

MAIDEN FLIGHT

Child.

Child
don't open out your eyes.
Feel for the nipple,
drink my milk
and sleep.

Dream the gyrations
of your life.
Dream ice and knives
of mountains sabring the sky; dream
nectarines and moths
with emerald wings. Batten
your eyelids down to see how mist
on a morning river cons time,
halts the train's whistle in mid note;
wraps up the heart in marble;
smiles light,
musics silence,
liquidizes stone.

In that conception you can fly
forever; hang from a branch
of a tree so old it knew a world
before the ape, before the crippled thing
turned the wheel into the barrel of a gun.

Sleep gentle, child;
sleep wild with passion
in a tropic night.
Dream till your breath
has had enough
and death will tuck you
in sleek wings.

DOWN DRAUGHT

Day falls;
the flat of light in windows,
dog star's fading grin.

The crippled thing stirs,
sips his tea; limps out
to make his rounds, mine
cretin's gold;
out of his tenements, shoddy palaces,
acrid back-to-backs, fouled semi-nests
and dungeons with herbaceous walls;
mounts his car
to haul dung, fell forests, piss
rivulets; spit wind.

Here in the cave, my child and I
my child, outsprung of thighs.
OK, a little sperm, a few laced genes,
but of my blood, teeth, flesh and bones;
calcification of my milk -

here in the warm dark
we hang
like cambrels

wait;

we and sky curving
buzzards, blow-flies,
ants.

WIND WHISPER

Child, your great grandmother
was a country girl; lived
in a barn with great white
ghostly owls; told such tales,
knew the seasons' warps,
the harvest feasts
among horse-flies.

But you must shape your flight
to other worlds - not hers,
not mine
When my bones are picked,
my wings are webs
and you have drawn
a man's sting, left him dead,
you'll nurse your daughter
to another music's beat,
shield her
from the greed of light.

SOFT LANDING

Now the wisp hour
in the dene,
leaf still.
Now the dream.

Silk sable tendrils
on the hills;
owl song, throb
of glutted toads, whispering
of our tribe's parchment wings.

Now the child time, daughter,
feel the summer's air on fur;
drink dew that floats
above the lily's smile;
feed on fireflies
under a lace-veiled moon.